Fire of Love!

Understanding Purgatory

by

St. Catherine of Genoa

SOPHIA INSTITUTE PRESS®

Manchester, New Hampshire

Fire of Love! Understanding Purgatory is a revision of the translation made of St. Catherine's treatise on Purgatory begun by Charlotte Balfour in the nineteenth century and completed by Helen Douglas Irvine in the twentieth. That work was published in 1946 by Sheed and Ward in London under the title *Treatise on Purgatory: The Dialogue.*

Sophia Institute Press

Box 5284, Manchester, NH 03108

1-800-888-9344

Library of Congress Cataloging-in-Publication Data

Catherine, of Genoa, Saint, 1447-1510.
　　[Trattato del Purgatorio. English]
　　Fire of love! : understanding Purgatory / St. Catherine of Genoa.
　　　　p. cm.
　　"Fire of love! is a revision of the translation . . . which was published in 1946 by Sheed and Ward in London under the title Treatise on Purgatory: The Dialogue" — P.
　　ISBN: 0-918477-41-7 (pbk. : alk. paper)
　　1. Purgatory — Early works to 1800.   I. Title.
BT840.C3313　1996
234'.5—dc20　　　　　　　　　　96-12881
　　　　　　　　　　　　　　　　　CIP

97 98 99 00 01 9 8 7 6 5 4 3

Contents

Introduction

St. Catherine
and Her Works

Caterinetta Fieschi was born in 1447 to an aristocratic family in the great Italian seaport of Genoa. Spiritually precocious from childhood, Catherine tried to enter an Augustinian convent when she was thirteen, but was refused because of her age.[1]

A few years later her father died, and in the aftermath, her elder brother sought to promote the family fortunes by espousing Catherine to Giuliano Adorno, a member of another aristocratic Genoese family. Submitting to the wishes of her family, Catherine married Giuliano at age sixteen in 1463, but the marriage was unhappy due to Giuliano's infidelity and financial irresponsibility.

For the first five years of her married life, depressed at her situation, Catherine withdrew

---

[1] For additional information on St. Catherine's life and thought, the reader may consult Benedict J. Groeschel, introduction to Catherine of Genoa, *Purgation and Purgatory; The Spiritual Dialogue,* trans. Serge Hughes (New York: Paulist Press, 1979), 1-43.

from the social life of the city. Then, encouraged by her family, she spent another five years trying to adjust to the prescribed role of an affluent young wife in Genoese society, an effort that led to increasing frustration and dissatisfaction.

Catherine's life was changed completely when she underwent a profound conversion in 1473. For several months, convinced of her appalling sinfulness, she experienced intense recollection in prayer and practiced many severe penances. During this same time, however, she began to go out into the city streets of Genoa to serve the poor there. Simultaneously, Catherine's husband Giuliano, who by now was financially bankrupt, also underwent conversion and became a Third-Order Franciscan. Now reconciled, Catherine and Giuliano agreed to a celibate marriage and moved to a small house near the large Pammatone Hospital in Genoa. There they devoted themselves without salary to caring for the patients.

After the first few years of her conversion passed, Catherine lost her preoccupation with her own sinfulness and abandoned the severe penances she had been practicing. Instead, she developed a great devotion to the Eucharist, and in May 1474 was granted permission to receive Communion daily, a rare privilege at the time.

Catherine also continued to manifest unusual spiritual gifts. From March 1476 to 1499, she fasted completely during Advent and Lent, and again, in the late 1470s, she began to experience spiritual ecstasies in which she received many of the insights that she later revealed to her associates in her teachings.

Despite these mysterious gifts, Catherine continued her work at the Pammatone with full vigor and ever increasing compassion. In 1479, Catherine and Giuliano moved into the hospital, and in 1490, Catherine was appointed Director, a post she held until 1496. Catherine was in charge of the hospital during the disastrous plague of 1493, during which four-fifths of the citizens who had remained in Genoa perished. Later that year, Giuliano died.

Fire of Love!

In the years after she relinquished the director-ship of the Pammatone, Catherine continued to work at the hospital. She also began to speak to her associates about the things revealed to her in ecstatic prayer. These teachings were later written down by her admirers and transmitted in two trea-tises, *On Purgation and Purgatory* (published here as *Fire of Love!*) and *The Spiritual Dialogue.*

After several years of declining health, Cather-ine died on September 15, 1510. Buried in the hospital's chapel, her body was found to be per-fectly intact eighteen months later when repairs to the building were being done. It continues incorrupt today. Pope Clement XII canonized Catherine in 1733. Her feast is September 15.

The influence of St. Catherine

Admired as much for her competence as a lov-ing and efficient hospital administrator as for her mystical transports, St. Catherine of Genoa and her teachings have enjoyed considerable influence in many quarters of the Christian world.

During St. Catherine's lifetime, and under her influence, one of her admirers, Ettore Vernazza, founded the Oratory of Divine Love, a group of clerics and laymen devoted to reform of the Church through spiritual reform of individuals and care of the poor.

Later, St. Catherine's heroic example in serving the poor and the sick inspired St. Aloysius Gonzaga, the Jesuit novice and patron saint of Catholic youth, who died caring for plague victims in Rome in 1591.

St. Catherine's mystical doctrine, contained in *The Spiritual Dialogue,* is thought to have influenced the great Spanish mystic St. John of the Cross. St. Francis de Sales enjoyed quoting from the *Life* of St. Catherine, composed shortly after her death. St. Catherine is also believed to have influenced the French Oratorian and Carmelite movements. Through the former, she influenced St. Vincent de Paul.

Interestingly, in the nineteenth century, St. Catherine's influence is traceable in Protestant

as well as Catholic circles. At the beginning of the
century, the founder of German Romanticism,
Frederick von Schlegel, translated *The Spiritual
Dialogue.* In England, the Anglican converts to
Catholicism Cardinal Manning, Frederick Faber,
and Cardinal Newman all read the treatises con-
taining St. Catherine's doctrine and incorporated
it in their own writings, Cardinal Newman most
pointedly in his poem *The Dream of Gerontius.*

In the United States, St. Catherine provided
a focus of interest for Protestant Christians in the
Congregationalist and Methodist traditions, who
regarded her as a role model for Christians and
one that proved that perfection was attainable in
the lay state. Also in America, the Redemptorist
priest and founder of the Paulist order, Fr. Isaac
Hecker, was a great admirer of St. Catherine, seeing in her the perfect foil to those who claimed
that Catholicism promotes a mechanical piety or
fosters a sanctity unconcerned with the real needs
of suffering humanity in society. To the latter
charge he replied forcefully:

St. Catherine and Her Works

"Read the life of St. Catherine, and in imagination fancy her in the city hospital of Genoa, charged not only with the supervision and responsibility of its finances, but also overseeing the care of its sick inmates, taking an active, personal part in its duties as one of its nurses, and conducting the whole establishment with strict economy, perfect order, and the tenderest care and love!

Fancy this for a moment in the city hospital of Genoa in the sixteenth century, and seek for her compeer in the city of New York, or in any other city in the world, in our day, and if you find one, and outside of the Catholic Church, then, but not till then, you may repeat to your heart's content that She fosters a sanctity which turns one's attention away from this world, and makes one indifferent to the wants of humanity."[2]

[2] I. T. Hecker, *The Church and the Age* (New York: Office of the Catholic World, 1887), 176-177.

Fire of Love!

In this century the great English scholar of mysticism, Evelyn Underhill, has spoken glowingly of St. Catherine as one "whose inner and outer lives in their balanced wholeness provide us with one of our best standards by which to judge the right proportions of the Mystic Way."[3]

St. Catherine of Genoa's life combined the noblest forms of Christian service with the highest levels of contemplative prayer. May her life and her doctrine help us, too, to live out our Christian discipleship, inspired by the love of God she taught and exemplified.

Her treatise "On Purgation and Purgatory"

Communicated to her disciples toward the end of her life, the insights about Purgatory that St. Catherine received in prayer were later written down as a treatise entitled *On Purgation and Purgatory* (which we have retitled *Fire of Love!*).

[3] Evelyn Underhill, *Mysticism: A Study in the Nature and Development of Man's Spiritual Consciousness* (Cleveland: The World Publishing Co., 1955), 441.

This treatise constitutes an important contribution to Christian eschatology, the Church's doctrine of the "last things." A teaching with deep roots in biblical and patristic tradition, the Church definitively taught the existence of Purgatory at councils in Lyons in 1245 and 1274, and again at the Council of Florence in 1439-1444. However, doubts caused by the sale of indulgences as well as heavy emphasis on the punitive dimensions of Purgatory led many late medieval Christians to question the doctrine of Purgatory. The newly emergent Protestant churches even rejected it outright.

St. Catherine's remarkable teachings on Purgatory counter this trend, showing how Purgatory is an essential element of our love for God and of His love for us.

For Catherine, the most important aspect of the Church's teaching on Purgatory is not suffering *per se*, but on God's loving will, which inspires the faithful soul joyfully to embrace suffering in this life as well as in Purgatory, so that it may be purged of all imperfection discordant with God's goodness.

For those readers who may only be familiar with Purgatory as one of the Catholic Church's more vague — and disturbing — doctrines, St. Catherine's teaching demonstrates how integral this doctrine is to the Christian understanding of God's love for humankind and to the latter's response to this love. St. Catherine's insights on Purgatory enable Christians to face the sorrows of this life and the next with more courage and trust, confident that suffering serves their further perfection and eventual union with their all-loving Creator.

May publication of this brief treatise on purgation and Purgatory introduce a new generation of Christians to this exemplary saint and her luminous, hopeful teaching on spiritual purification as the fruit of God's love come to maturity in the human heart — now, after death, and through all eternity.

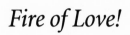

Fire of Love!

1

Charity
in Purgatory

This holy soul found herself, while still in the flesh, placed by the fiery love of God in Purgatory, which burnt her, cleansing whatever in her needed cleansing, to the end that when she passed from this life she might be presented to the sight of God, her dear love.

By means of this loving fire, she understood in her soul the state of the souls of the faithful who are placed in Purgatory to purge them of all the rust and stains of sin of which they have not rid themselves in this life.

And since this soul, placed by the divine fire in this loving Purgatory, was united to that divine love and content with all that was wrought in her, she understood the state of the souls who are in Purgatory. And she said:

The souls who are in Purgatory cannot, as I understand, choose but be there, and this is by the ordinance of God, who therein has done justly.

They cannot turn their thoughts back to themselves, nor can they say, 'Such sins I have committed for which I deserve to be here,' nor, 'I wish that

I had not committed them for then I would go now to Paradise,' nor, 'That person will leave sooner than I' nor 'I will leave sooner than he.' They can have no memory either of themselves nor of others, whether of good or evil, as a result of which they would have greater pain than they suffer ordinarily.

So happy are they to be within God's ordinance, and that He should do all that pleases Him *as* it pleases Him, that in their greatest pain they cannot think of themselves. They see only the working of the divine goodness, which leads man to itself mercifully, so that he no longer sees anything of the pain or good that may befall him. Nor would these souls be in pure charity if they could see that pain or good. They cannot see that they are in pain because of their sins; that sight they cannot hold in their minds because in it there would be an active imperfection, which cannot be where no actual sin exists.

Only once, as they pass from this life, do souls see the cause of the Purgatory they endure; never again do they see it, for in another sight of it there would be self. Being then in charity, from which they cannot now depart by any actual fault, they can no longer will or desire save with the pure will of pure charity. Being in that fire of Purgatory, they are within the divine ordinance, which is pure charity, and in nothing can they depart from it, for they are deprived of the power to sin as they are of the power to merit.

2

Happiness
in Purgatory

I believe no happiness can be found worthy to be compared with that of a soul in Purgatory except that of the saints in Paradise. And day by day this happiness grows as God flows into these souls, more and more as the hindrance to His entrance is consumed. Sin's rust is the hindrance, and the fire burns the rust away so that more and more the soul opens itself up to the divine inflowing.

A thing that is covered cannot respond to the sun's rays, not because of any defect in the sun, which is shining all the time, but because the cover is an obstacle; if the cover be burnt away, this thing is open to the sun; more and more as the cover is consumed does it respond to the rays of the sun.

It is in this way that rust, which is sin, covers souls, and in Purgatory is burnt away by fire; the more it is consumed, the more do souls respond to God, the true sun. As the rust lessens and the soul is opened up to the divine rays, happiness grows. Until the time be accomplished, the one wanes and the other waxes. However, pain does not lessen but only the time for which pain is endured. As for the will, the souls can never say these pains are pains, so contented are they with God's ordaining with which, in pure charity, their will is united.

But, on the other hand, the souls in Purgatory endure a pain so extreme that no tongue can be found to tell it, nor could the mind understand its least pang if God, by a special grace, did not reveal this to it.

And the least pang of this pain God of His grace did show to this soul, but with her tongue she cannot say what it is. This sight that the Lord revealed to me has never since left my mind and I will tell what I can of it. Those whose mind God deigns to open will understand.

3

Our Need
for Purgatory

All the pains of Purgatory arise from original or actual sin. God created the soul pure, simple, and clean of all stain of sin, with a certain beatific instinct towards Himself. Original sin, which the soul finds in itself, draws it away from this instinct; and when actual sin is added to original sin, the soul is drawn yet further away. The further it departs from its beatific instinct, the more malignant it becomes because it is less conformed to God.

There can be no good save by participation in God, who meets the needs of irrational creatures as He wills and has ordained, never failing them, and who answers a rational soul in the measure in which He finds it cleansed of sin's hindrance.

Therefore when a soul has come near to the pure and clear state in which it was created, its beatific instinct asserts itself and grows unceasingly, so impetuously and with such fierce charity (drawing the soul to its last end) that any hindrance seems to this soul a thing past bearing. The more it sees, the more extreme is its pain.

Fire of Love!

Because the souls in Purgatory are without the guilt of sin, there is no hindrance between them and God except their pain, which holds them back so that they cannot reach perfection. Clearly they see the grievousness of every least hindrance in their way. They also see that their instinct is hindered by a necessity of justice. From this understanding is born a raging fire, like that of Hell save that guilt is lacking to it.

It is guilt that makes the will of the damned in Hell malignant, on whom God does not bestow His goodness and who therefore remain in desperate ill will, opposed to the will of God.

4

Repentance
in Purgatory

Hence it is manifest that there is perversity of will, contrary to the will of God, where the guilt is known and ill will persists, and that the guilt of those who have passed with ill will from this life to Hell is not remitted. Nor can this guilt ever be remitted since these souls may no longer change the will with which they have passed out of this life, for in this passage the soul is made stable in good or evil in accordance with its deliberate will.

As it is written in Scripture, "Where I shall find you," — that is, in the hour of death, with the will to sin or with dissatisfaction with sin or with repentance for sin — "there I shall judge you."[4] And of this judgment there is afterwards no remission, as I will show.

After death free will can never return, for the will is fixed as it was at the moment of death. Because the souls in Hell were found at the moment of death to have in them the will to sin,

[4] Cf. Eccles. 11:3.

they bear the guilt throughout eternity, suffering not indeed the pains they deserve but such pains as they endure, and these without end.

But the souls in Purgatory bear only pain, for their guilt was wiped away at the moment of their death when they were found to be ill content with their sins and repentant for their offenses against divine goodness. Therefore their pain is finite and its time ever lessening, as has been said.

Oh, misery beyond all other misery, the greater because human blindness does not take it into account!

The pain of the damned is not infinite in quantity because the dear goodness of God sheds the ray of His mercy even in Hell. For the man who is dead in sin merits infinite pain for an infinite time, but God's mercy has allotted infinity to him only in time and has limited the quantity of his pain; in justice God could have given him more pain.

Oh, how dangerous is sin committed in malice! Rarely does a man repent of it, and without repentance he will bear its guilt for as long as he perseveres — that is, for as long as he wills a sin committed or wills to sin again.

5

God's Will
in Purgatory

The souls in Purgatory have wills accordant in all things with the will of God, who therefore sheds on them His goodness, and they, as far as their will goes, are happy and cleansed of all their sin.

As for guilt, these cleansed souls are as they were when God created them, for God immediately forgives the guilt of those who have passed from this life ill content with their sins, having confessed all they have committed and having the will to commit no more. Only the rust of sin is left them and from this they cleanse themselves by pain in the fire. Thus cleansed of all guilt and united in will to God, they see Him clearly in the degree to which He makes Himself known to them, and see, too, how essential it is to enjoy Him and that souls have been created for this end.

Moreover, these souls are brought to a conformity with God that unites them to Him to such a degree, and are drawn to Him in such a way, His natural instinct towards souls working in them, that neither arguments nor figures nor examples

Fire of Love!

can make the thing clear as the mind knows it to
be in reality and as by inner feeling it is understood to be. I will, however, make one comparison
that comes to my mind.

6

Spiritual Hunger
in Purgatory

If in all the world there were but one loaf of bread to feed the hunger of all creatures, and if they were satisfied by the sight of it alone, then since man, if he is healthy, has an instinct to eat, his hunger, if he neither ate nor sickened nor died, would grow unceasingly, for his instinct to eat would not lessen. Knowing that there was only that loaf to satisfy him and that without it he must remain hungry, he would be in unbearable pain.

All the more would his natural craving for this loaf be strengthened if he went near it and could not see it. His instinct would fix his desire wholly on that loaf, which held everything that could content him.

At this point, if he were sure he would never see the loaf again, he would be in Hell.

Thus are the souls of the damned from whom has been taken any hope of ever seeing their bread, which is God the true Savior.

But the souls in Purgatory have the hope of seeing their bread and of wholly satisfying themselves with it. Therefore they suffer hunger and endure

Fire of Love!

pain in that measure in which they will be able
to satisfy themselves with the bread that is Jesus
Christ, true God and Savior and our Love.

7

Hell
and Purgatory

As the clean and purified spirit can find rest only in God, having been created for this end, so there is no place save Hell for the soul in sin, for whose end Hell was ordained by God. When the soul is in mortal sin as it leaves the body, then in the instant in which spirit and body are separated, the soul goes to the place ordained for it, guided by nothing save the nature of its sin. And if at that moment the soul were bound by no ordinance proceeding from God's justice, it would go to a yet greater Hell than that in which it abides, for it would be outside His ordinance, in which divine mercy so disposes that God gives the soul less pain than it deserves. The soul, finding no other place at hand nor any holding less evil for it, casts itself by God's ordinance into Hell as into its proper place.

Let us return to our subject, which is the Purgatory of the soul separated from the body when it is no longer clean as it was created. Seeing in itself the impediment that can be taken away only by means of Purgatory, the soul casts itself therein swiftly and willingly. Were there not the ordinance it thus obeys, one suitable to rid it of its encumbrance, the soul would in that instant beget within itself a Hell worse than Purgatory, for it would see that because of that impediment it could not draw near to God, its end. So essential is God to the soul that, in comparison, Purgatory counts for nothing, even though it is like Hell, as has been said. But compared to God, it appears as almost nothing.

8

Mercy
in Purgatory

When I look at God, I see no gate to Paradise, and yet he who wishes to enter there does so, because God is all mercy. God stands before us with open arms to receive us into His glory. But well I see the divine essence to be of such purity, far greater than can be imagined, that the soul in which there is even the least note of imperfection would rather cast itself into a thousand Hells than find itself thus stained in the presence of the Divine Majesty. Therefore the soul, understanding that Purgatory has been ordained to take away those stains, casts itself therein, and seems to itself to have found great mercy in that it can rid itself there of the impediment that is the stain of sin.

No tongue can tell nor explain, no mind under-stand, the grievousness of Purgatory. But although I see that there is in Purgatory as much pain as in Hell, I yet see the soul that has the least stain of imperfection accepting Purgatory as though it were a mercy, as I have said, and holding its pains of no account as compared with the least stain

Fire of Love!

that hinders a soul in its love. I seem to see that the pain that souls in Purgatory endure because of that in them which displeases God (that is, what they have willfully done against His great goodness) is greater than any other pain they feel in Purgatory. And this is because they see the truth and the grievousness of the hindrance that prevents them from drawing near to God, since they are in grace.

9

The Fire of Love
in Purgatory

All these things, which I have securely in mind to the extent that in this life I have been able to understand them, are, compared with what I have said, extremely great. Beside them, all the sights and sounds and justice and truths of this world seem to me lies and nothingness. I am left confused because I cannot find words extreme enough for these things.

I perceive there to be so much conformity between God and the soul that when He sees it in the purity in which His Divine Majesty created it, He gives it a burning love, which draws it to Himself, which is strong enough to destroy it, immortal though it be, and which causes it to be so transformed in God that it sees itself as though it were none other than God. Unceasingly God draws the soul to Himself and breathes fire into it, never letting it go until He has led it to the state from which it came forth — that is, to the pure cleanliness in which it was created.

When with its inner sight the soul sees itself drawn by God with such loving fire, then it is melted by the heat of the glowing love for God its most dear Lord, which it feels overflowing it. And it sees by the divine light that God does not cease drawing it, nor from leading it, lovingly and with much care and unfailing foresight, to its full perfection, doing this out of His pure love. But the soul, because it is hindered by sin, cannot go where God draws it; it cannot follow the uniting look by which God would draw it to Himself. Again the soul perceives the grievousness of being held back from seeing the divine light; the soul's instinct, too, since it is drawn by that uniting look, craves to be unhindered.

I say that it is the sight of these things that begets in the souls the pain they feel in Purgatory. Not that they make account of their pain; although it is most great, they deem it a far less evil than to find themselves going against the will of God, whom they clearly see to be on fire with extreme and pure love for them.

Strongly and unceasingly this love draws the soul with that uniting look, as though it had nothing else than this to do. Could the soul who understood this find a worse Purgatory in which to rid itself sooner of all the hindrance in its way, it would swiftly fling itself therein, driven by the conforming love between itself and God.

10

Purification
in Purgatory

I see, too, certain rays and shafts of light that go out from that divine love towards the soul, and are penetrating and strong enough to seem as though they must destroy not only the body but the soul, too, were that possible. Two works are wrought by these rays: the first is purification and the second is destruction.

Look at gold: the more you melt it, the better it becomes; you could melt it until you had destroyed in it every imperfection. Thus does fire work on material things.

The soul cannot be destroyed insofar as it is in God, but insofar as it is in itself it can be destroyed; the more it is purified, the more the self is destroyed within it, until at last it is pure in God.

When gold has been purified up to twenty-four carats, it can no longer be consumed by any fire; not the gold itself but only dross can be burnt away. Thus the divine fire works in the soul: God holds the soul in the fire until its every imperfection is burnt away and it is brought to perfection,

Fire of Love!

as it were, to the purity of twenty-four carats —
each soul, however, according to its own degree.

When the soul has been purified it remains
wholly in God, having nothing of the self in it; its
being is in God, who has led this cleansed soul to
Himself. The soul can suffer no more, for nothing
is left in it to be burnt away. Were it held in the
fire when it has thus been cleansed, it would feel
no pain. Rather the fire of divine love would be
to it like eternal life and in no way contrary to it.

11

Sins Revealed
in Purgatory

The soul was created as well prepared as it can be for reaching perfection, if it lives as God has ordained and does not foul itself with any stain of sin. But having fouled itself by original sin, the soul loses its gifts and graces and lies dead, nor can it rise again save by God's means. And when God, by Baptism, has raised it from the dead, the soul is still prone to evil, inclining and being led to actual sin unless it resists. And thus it dies again.

Then God by another special grace raises the soul again, yet it stays so sullied and so turned to self that all the divine workings of which we have spoken are needed to recall it to the first state in which God created it. Without them the soul could never get back to that state.

And when the soul finds itself on the road back to its first state, its need to be transformed in God kindles in it a fire so great that this is its Purgatory. Not that it can look upon this as Purgatory, but its instinct to God, aflame and thwarted, makes Purgatory.

Fire of Love!

A last act of love is done by God without any help from man. So many hidden imperfections are in the soul that, if it saw them, it would live in despair. But in the state of which we have spoken they are all burnt away, and only when they are gone does God show them to the soul, so that it may see the divine working that kindles the fire of love in which its imperfections have been burnt away.

12

Happiness
in Purgatory

Know that what man deems perfection in himself is in God's sight faulty. For all the things a man does, which he sees or feels or means or wills or remembers to have a perfect appearance, are wholly fouled and sullied unless he acknowledges them to be from God. If a work is to be perfect it must be wrought *in* us but not chiefly *by* us, for God's works must be done by Him and not wrought chiefly by man.

The works wrought in us by God out of His pure and immaculate love, by Him alone without merit of ours are great, and so penetrating are they and such fire do they kindle in the soul, that the body that wraps it seems to be consumed as in a furnace, never to be quenched until death.

It is true that the love for God, which fills the soul to overflowing, as I see it, gives it a happiness beyond what can be told. And yet this happiness takes not one pang from the pain of the souls in Purgatory.

Rather the love of these souls, finding itself hindered, causes their pain; and the more perfect

Fire of Love!

the love of which God has made them capable,
the greater is their pain.

So the souls in Purgatory enjoy the greatest
happiness and endure the greatest pain; the one
does not hinder the other.

13

Justice
in Purgatory

I f the souls in Purgatory could purge themselves by contrition, they would pay all their
debt in one instant, such blazing vehemence
would their contrition have in the clear light shed
for them on the grievousness of being hindered
from reaching their end and the love of God.

Know surely that not the least bit of payment
is remitted to those souls, for thus has it been
determined by God's justice. So much for what
God does; as for what souls do, they can no longer
choose for themselves, nor can they see or will,
save as God wills, for thus has it been determined
for them.

And if any alms be done for the souls in Purgatory to lessen the time of their pain by those who
are in the world, they cannot turn with affection
to contemplate the deed, except as it is weighed in
the most just scales of the divine will. They leave
all in the hands of God, who is paid as His infinite
goodness pleases. If they could turn to contemplate the alms other than as they are within the
divine will, there would be self in what they did

Fire of Love!

and they would lose sight of God's will, which would make a Hell for them. Therefore they await immovably all that God gives them, whether pleasure and happiness or pain, and never again can they turn their eyes back to themselves.

14

Contentment
in Purgatory

S o intimate with God are the souls in Purgatory and so conformed to His will, that in all things they are content with His most holy ordinance.

And if a soul were brought to see God when it still had the smallest thing of which to purge itself, a great injury would be done to it. For since pure love and supreme justice could not brook that stained soul, and to bear with its presence would not befit God, that soul would suffer a torment worse than ten Purgatories. To see God when full satisfaction had not yet been given to Him, even if the time of purgation lacked but the twinkling of an eye, would be unbearable to the soul. It would sooner go to a thousand Hells to rid itself of the little rust still clinging to it, than stand in the divine presence when it was not yet wholly cleansed.

15

A Warning
from Purgatory

And so that blessed soul, seeing the aforesaid things by the divine light, said: I would willingly send up a cry so loud that it would put fear in all men on the earth. I would say to them: Wretches, why do you let yourselves be thus blinded by the world, you whose need is so great and grievous (as you will know at the moment of death) and who make no provision for it whatsoever?

You have all taken shelter beneath hope in God's mercy, which is, you say, very great, but you do not see that this great goodness of God will judge you for having gone against the will of so good a Lord. His goodness should compel you to do *all* His will, not give you hope in ill-doing, for His justice cannot fail, but in one way or another must be fully satisfied.

Cease to hug yourselves, saying: 'I will confess my sins and then receive plenary indulgence, and at that moment I shall be purged of all my sins and thus shall be saved.' Think of the confession and the contrition that are needed for that plenary

Fire of Love!

indulgence, so rarely achieved that, if you knew,
you would tremble in great fear, more sure that
you would never win it than that you ever could.

16

Joyful Suffering
in Purgatory

I see that the souls who suffer the pains of Purgatory have before their eyes two works of God.

First, they see themselves suffering pain willingly, and as they consider their own deserts and acknowledge how they have grieved God, it seems to them that He has shown them great mercy. For if His goodness had not tempered justice with mercy, making satisfaction with the precious blood of Jesus Christ, one sin would deserve a thousand perpetual Hells. Therefore the souls in Purgatory suffer pain willingly, and would not lighten it by one pang, knowing that they most fully deserve it and that it has been well ordained, and they no more complain of God, as far as their will goes, than if they were in eternal life.

The second work seen by the souls in Purgatory is the happiness they feel as they contemplate God's ordinance and the love and mercy with which He works on the soul.

In one instant God imprints these two visions on their minds, and because they are in grace, they are aware of these visions and understand them as they are, in the measure of their capacity.

Thus a great happiness is granted them that never fails; rather it grows as they draw nearer to God. These souls see these visions neither in nor of themselves but in God, on whom they are far more intent than on the pains they suffer, and of whom they make far greater account, beyond all comparison, than of their pains.

For every glimpse that can be had of God exceeds any pain or joy a man can feel. However, although it exceeds the pain and joy of these souls, such a glimpse does not lessen them by the tiniest bit.

17

Purgatory
Suffered in This Life

This form of purgation, which I see in the souls in Purgatory, I feel in my own mind. In the last two years I have felt it most; every day I feel and see it more clearly. I see my soul within this body as in a purgatory, formed as is the true Purgatory and like it, but so measured that the body can bear with it and not die; yet little by little it grows until the body dies.

I see my spirit estranged from all things that can feed it, even spiritual things, such as gaiety, delight, and consolation, and without the power to enjoy anything, spiritual or temporal, by will or mind or memory, so that I might say one thing contents me more than another.

Inwardly I find myself besieged, as it were. All things by which spiritual or bodily life is refreshed have, little by little, been taken from my inner self, which knows, now that they are gone, that they fed and comforted me.

But so hateful and abhorrent are these things, as they are known to the spirit, that they all go, never to return. This is because of the spirit's

instinct to rid itself of whatever hinders its perfection; so ruthless is the spirit that to fulfill its
purpose it would all but cast itself into Hell.
Therefore it ever deprives the inner man of all
on which it can feed, besieging it so cunningly
that it lets not the least atom of imperfection
pass unseen and unabhorred.

As for my outer man, since the spirit does not
respond to it, it, too, is so besieged that it finds
nothing to refresh it on the earth if it follows its
human instinct. No comfort is left it save God,
who works all this by love and very mercifully
in satisfaction of His justice. To perceive this gives
my outer man great peace and happiness, but
happiness that neither lessens my pain nor weak-
ens the siege.

Yet no pain could ever be inflicted on me so
great that I would wish to depart from the divine
ordinance. I neither leave my prison nor seek to
go forth from it: let God do what is needed! My
happiness is that God be satisfied, nor could I
suffer a worse pain than that of going outside

God's ordinance, so just do I see Him to be and so very merciful.

All these things of which I have spoken are what I see and, as it were, touch, but I cannot find fit words to say about them as much as I would like. Nor can I say rightly what I have told of the work done in me, which I have felt spiritually. I have tried to tell it, however.

The world is the prison in which I seem to be, my chains the body, and it is my soul enlightened by grace that knows the grievousness of being held down or kept back and thus hindered from pursuing its end.

This gives my soul great pain, for it is very tender. By God's grace it receives a certain dignity that makes it like unto God; nay, rather He lets my soul share His goodness so that it becomes one with Him.

Since it is impossible that God suffer pain, this immunity, too, befalls the souls who draw near Him; the nearer they come, the more they partake of what is His.

Fire of Love!

Therefore to be hindered on its way, as it is, causes the soul unbearable pain. The pain and the hindrance wrest it from its first natural state, which by grace is revealed to it, and finding itself deprived of what it is able to receive, it suffers greater or lesser pain according to the measure of its esteem for God. The more the soul knows God, the more it esteems Him and the more sinless it becomes, so that the hindrance in its way grows yet more terrible to it, above all because the soul that is unhindered and wholly recollected in God knows Him as He truly is.

As the man who would let himself be killed rather than offend God feels death and its pain, but is given by the light of God a zeal that causes him to esteem divine honor above bodily death, so the soul who knows God's ordinance esteems it above all possible inner and outer torments, terrible though they may be, for this is a work of God, who surpasses all that can be felt or imagined.

Moreover, when God occupies a soul, in however small a degree, He keeps it wholly occupied with His majesty so that nothing else counts for it. Thus the soul loses all that is its own, and can of itself neither see nor speak, nor know loss or pain. But, as I have already said clearly, it knows all in one instant when it leaves this life.

Finally and in conclusion, let us understand that God, who is best and greatest, causes all that is of man to be lost, and that Purgatory cleanses it away.